Explorers and Mapmakers

by Peter Ryan

illustrated by Chris Molan
and with photographs

Evans Brothers Limited

Published by Evans Brothers Limited
2A Portman Mansions
Chiltern Street
London W1M 1LE

First published in Great Britain in 1989 by
Hamish Hamilton Children's Books

© Peter Ryan (text) 1989
© Chris Molan (illustrations) 1989

Maps and diagrams by Gillian Riley

Conceived, designed and produced by
Belitha Press Ltd,
31 Newington Green, London N16 9PU
© in this format Belitha Press Ltd 1989
Creative Director: Treld Bicknell
Designer: Gillian Riley
Editor: Felicity Trotman

Reprinted 1991, 1992

Printed in Hong Kong for Imago

ISBN 0 237 60275 X

The author and publishers wish to thank the following for
permission to reproduce copyright material:

The National Maritime Museum, title page (compass),
pp 18, 22 *both*, 23, 24, 40 *top*
Royal Geographical Society, title page (John Hanning
Speke), p 36 *top*
By courtesy of the board of Trustees of the Victoria and
Albert Museum, title page (dish), p 15 *top left*
The Bridgeman Art Library, p 8
University of Heidelberg, p 12 *bottom left*
Yale University Press, pp 12-13 *main spread*
Peter Ryan, pp 14, 15 *bottom right*

Servizio Beni Cultorali Del Commune Di Genova, p 16
Bibliotheca Medicea Laurenziana, p 20
Anthony Sheil Associates Ltd, p 26, photographed by
Anne-Christine Jacobsen
Aerofilms Limited, p 27
By courtesy of the Trustees of the British Museum, p 30 *top*
Robert Harding Picture Library, p 30 *bottom*
Mary Evans Picture Library, p 36 *bottom*
Peter Newark's Western Americana, p 40 *bottom*
La Trobe Collection, The State Library of Victoria, p 42
The Hulton Picture Company, p 43
Scott Polar Research Institute, p 44
Science Photo Library, p 45 *both*, p 46

Contents

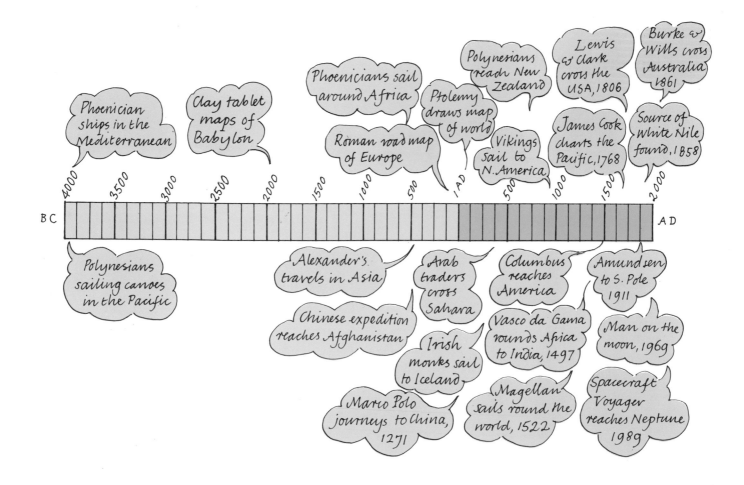

Introduction

If you do not know the way, you need a map.

Thousands of years ago, our ancestors lived in small family groups. They got their food by hunting wild animals and gathering wild plants. When they were looking for food, hunters had to remember directions and landmarks to find the way back to their families.

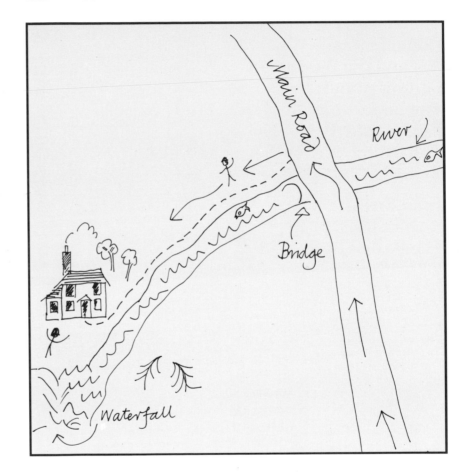

Say a friend invites you home for supper. You'll need to know the way.

Your friend says, 'Go down the road to the bridge over the river. Cross it and turn left. You will see a footpath which follows the river downstream. Follow the path until you come to a waterfall. My home is the white house next to it.'

Your friend has given you a few directions and landmarks. And you might draw a sketch map to make sure you remember them.

We can imagine everyone gathered round a fire. The hunters are safely home. A large meal has been cooked and eaten. One of the hunters is telling the story of the hunt, scratching the ground with a stick to show where they have been.

The first hunter to do this invented the map. A map made of scratchings on the ground does not last long, but then someone had the clever idea of drawing hunting trails on the skins of the animals they hunted.

FACT BOX

Early travellers used simple maps and landmarks to find their way from place to place. A landmark is an easily recognized and well-known part of a landscape, such as an unusually big tree or a pile of stones left as a way marker.

First Travellers

About ten thousand years ago, some of our ancestors became farmers. They caught animals they used to hunt, and planted seeds. On the banks of large rivers, they cleared fields and built shelters for their families and their flocks.

When they discovered clay for building houses and making pottery, and found out how to extract metal from ores, some of our ancestors became full-time craftsmen.

What they made in their workshops, the craftsmen traded for food from the farmers, or from the tribes which still lived by hunting.

Along the banks of the great rivers of Africa and Asia, the populations of the settlements grew.

Archaeologists have found remains of what these craftsmen made. Sometimes what is discovered is a long way from the workshop where it was made. This tells us that there was trade between settlements, and that some of our ancestors had become full-time traders.

Early human settlements were built in the valleys of big rivers.

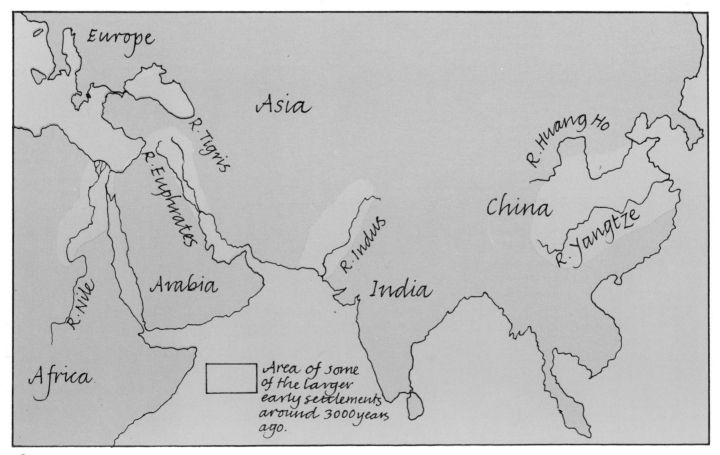

Area of some of the larger early settlements around 3000 years ago.

Maps and Directions

Guided by maps, drawn on animal skins or cloth, the traders journeyed from settlement to settlement, exchanging goods with farmers and craftsmen, and with the tribes of hunters and gatherers.

None of these maps has survived, so we have to guess what they were like. They were probably quite simple.

They showed roads to follow to get from settlement to settlement, and landmarks – drawn like signposts – to help prevent travellers from losing their way. These maps would show where water could be found, and caves in which travellers could find shelter.

Such maps showed where places were, but not how far one place was from another. So travellers probably asked other travellers how long it took to get from one place to another.

Then one day a mapmaker was looking at his thumb, and at the length of the first joint – the one with the thumbnail at the end. And on his map, the mapmaker used that small distance – the length of the first joint of a thumb – to show a large distance on the ground, say a thousand paces. This mapmaker invented *scale*. With the invention of scale, mapmakers could show how far one place is from another.

The captains of sea-going sailing ships use maps called charts to get from port to port. None of the earliest charts have survived, but they must have shown the mariners who used them landmarks along the coastline between ports, where there were safe places to anchor during storms, and where there were dangerous rocks.

With sailing ships and good charts, trade between settlements in Africa, Asia and Europe became much easier.

A mapmaker uses the length of the first joint of his thumb to show a larger distance on his map. He is using scale. Many maps include a drawing of the scale used to measure distances.

Ptolemy – an early Mapmaker

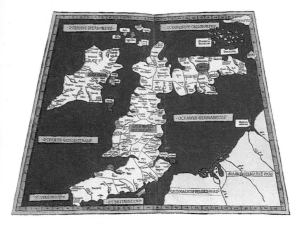

The ancient Greek mapmaker, Ptolemy, sits at his table, working on his map of the world. You might like to compare his drawing of Britain and Ireland—shown above—with a map of these two islands in a modern atlas.

The ancient Greeks were very good at measuring distances and using scale. One of them, a geographer from Alexandria called Ptolemy, began drawing a map of the world about 1800 years ago.

It was a difficult task. Traders often kept the routes of their journeys secret. Ptolemy had to persuade them to show him their maps and charts.

He succeeded. But no one could tell him that he had missed out two huge inhabited continents – America and Australia – and the vast Pacific Ocean which lies between them.

Unknown to Ptolemy, hunting and gathering tribes had long before reached America from the eastern end of Asia. Nor did he know of the Aborigines of Australia, or of the seafaring islanders of the Pacific.

Yet his map shows an extensive area of Europe, Asia, and the northern part of Africa. Much of Ptolemy's knowledge was later lost, and had to be rediscovered.

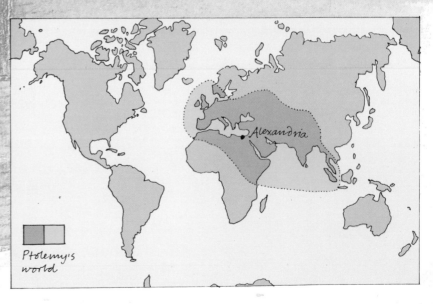

Ptolemy's map showed the parts of
the world known to the ancient Greeks.

1 Oceans and Seas: The Earliest Voyages

'There are three kinds of people: the living, the dead and those who sail the sea in ships.'

That was said by Anacharsis, a legendary sage of Scythia. He was commenting on the perils of travel by sea in ancient times, when mariners braved storm, shipwreck and starvation.

Many important maps have been drawn, and discoveries made, as a result of journeys by sea.

The first great seafarers came from two very different parts of the world – the coasts of the Mediterranean Sea and the Pacific Ocean. Their descendants would meet after many hundreds of years.

One ancient seafaring people, the Phoenicians, sailed out of the Mediterranean into the Atlantic Ocean to trade with Africa and the British Isles. They were one of the first peoples to sail voluntarily out of sight of land, which was a very brave thing to do.

The Polynesians of the Pacific sailed from island to island in ocean-going canoes.

Some say that in about 600 BC they sailed all the way round Africa, from the Red Sea to the Nile delta. And that is how the fifth century BC Greek historian Herodotus knew that Africa could be sailed round.

The Phoenicians depended on seafaring because as their numbers grew, they did not have enough land for farming in their rocky homeland at the eastern end of the Mediterranean. They got the extra food they needed by trading.

At the same time, another seafaring people, the Polynesians, were island hopping eastwards across the Pacific in large ocean-going sailing canoes. When one small island got too crowded, part of the population moved on to the next island. This meant covering enormous distances across the Pacific. By the ninth century AD the Polynesians found New Zealand and settled there. Eventually their Pacific island homeland covered a huge area – larger than that of any other people on earth.

Europe finds America

This map shows part of North America. The island on the left – called Vinland on this map – is part of what is now called Canada. This map was drawn before Columbus reached America. The old picture below shows Irish monks in a ship.

In the eighth century Irish monks were also looking for somewhere new to live. They built leather-covered boats called *curraghs*, and sailed north to Iceland. A century later, when their peace and quiet was disturbed by the arrival of the Vikings, the monks may have moved on to Greenland.

The Vikings were traders and raiders from Norway. They reached America before

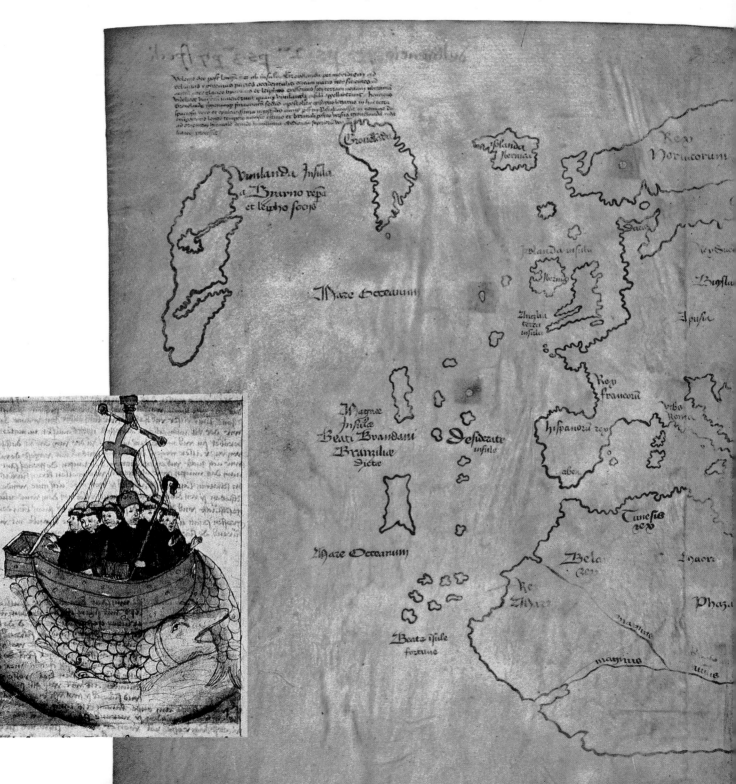

Christopher Columbus, but Columbus never realized this. Charts of Viking discoveries were unknown, or not believed, by the geographers of his time.

Our evidence is an old map. It shows part of North America, with a note about Viking discoveries. It was drawn by a Swiss monk in about 1440, fifty years before Columbus crossed the Atlantic.

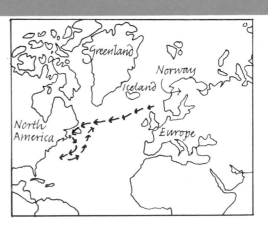

The Viking route from Europe to North America

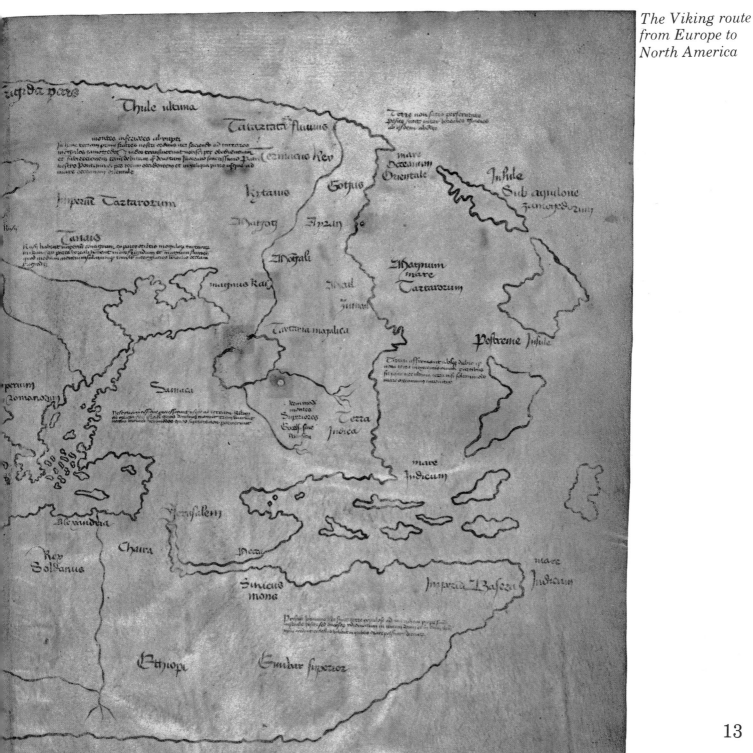

The Spice Trade

Columbus was an Italian-born sea captain who lived during what is now called the Age of Exploration. It began when European seafarers decided to sail to the edge of their charts.

Some people, thinking that the earth was flat, feared that these foolhardy explorers would fall off the edge of the world. But many seafarers believed that the world was round. And if it was round, why not sail round it?

The seafaring traders of the Atlantic coasts of Europe were keen to try. One very good reason was that they wanted to reach the spice markets of the Indies. That meant the spice-growing countries of India and Southeast Asia. Spices – pepper, cloves, cinnamon and nutmeg – were in huge demand. Try eating a meal with no salt, no pepper, nor any of the other ingredients that modern food companies put in their products. Spices make boring food taste better. Fortunes could be made by supplying them.

In the 1400s merchants from Europe traded spices for gold with merchants from the Indies. The photograph above shows spices in an Arabian market today. Some of the merchants' trade routes are shown in the map on the right.

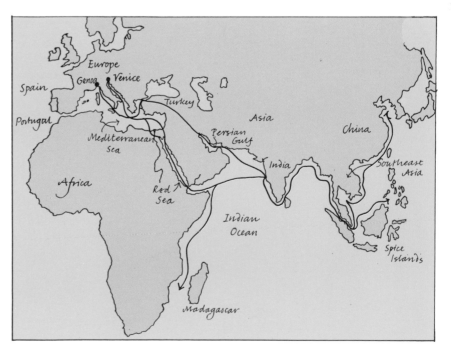

But the European end of the spice trade route was tightly controlled by rival Mediterranean traders, first by the Italian merchants of Venice and Genoa, later by the Turkish merchants of Constantinople, now called Istanbul.

Their fleets monopolized the sea routes to the eastern Mediterranean, where they traded with the Arabs.

With ocean-going wooden ships called *dhows*, Arab and Indian fleets controlled the sea routes up and down the Red Sea and the Persian Gulf and across the Indian Ocean to the western ports of India. And from there, the trade routes eastwards to the Indies were in the hands of not only the Arab merchants and fleets but those of India, Southeast Asia and China.

The merchants of Venice and Genoa could sell spices from the Indies to the merchants of other European cities for huge profits. A hundredweight of pepper cost only three Venetian ducats in the Indian port of Calicut, but was worth eighty ducats in Venice.

This did not please the rulers and merchants of Portugal and Spain. They asked their navigators to find another route to the Indies and its spices. They were also interested in finding sources of precious metal. Gold and silver to make coins were very scarce in Europe, and without plenty of money, trade and finance could not develop properly.

Strong wooden sailing ships were used for the spice trade. The painted plate above shows an old Portuguese ship. In the photograph below, a dhow *builder from Bangladesh holds a model of a sailing ship that is still in use today.*

Around the World

The Portuguese navigator Ferdinand Magellan.

From the Atlantic coast of Central America, in September 1513, the Spanish explorer Vasco de Balboa crossed the land at its narrowest point. When he reached the other side, he found himself on the shores of a huge ocean. He claimed it for Spain.

Seven years later, a Spanish expedition sailed through the dangerous, stormy straits at the extreme southern tip of South America into this new ocean. The new ocean was calm. So the captain, Ferdinand Magellan, a Portuguese

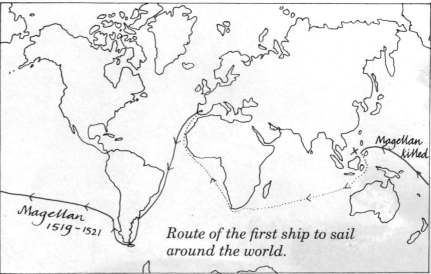

Magellan killed

Magellan 1519 - 1521

Route of the first ship to sail around the world.

navigator working for Spain called it *Pacific*, or peaceful ocean.

Magellan crossed the Pacific in ninety-eight days. In March 1521 he reached the Philippines but was killed in a battle between two island tribes. He had left Spain in 1519 with five old ships. Only one, the *Victoria*, returned home. Sailing into the Spanish port of Seville in 1522, the *Victoria* became the first ship to sail round the world. Of the 280 men who set sail with Magellan, thirty-five got home. The sailors suffered greatly. 'We ate only old biscuit turned to powder, all full of worms.... We ate also ox hides.... And of the rats ... some of us could not get enough.' The boats leaked and they had little water. Hunger, thirst, diseases – including the mariner's plague, scurvy – and hostile peoples all took lives.

But the rewards were high. The cargo of cloves and other spices brought back by the *Victoria* paid for the whole expedition.

Magellan had proved it was possible to reach the Indies from Spain by sailing west. But it was twice the expected distance. The Portuguese route to the east, round Africa, was shorter.

FACT BOX

Scurvy is a disease caused by a lack of vitamin C. Most of us get enough vitamin C by eating fresh fruit. Early explorers did not know about vitamins. On long journeys they had no fruit or vegetables to eat and so many fell ill with scurvy.

Sailing round Africa

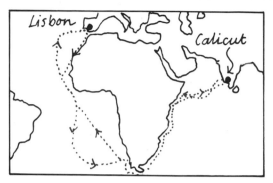

The Portuguese route from Europe to India, above. One of the earliest maps of the coasts of Africa and India, below. It also shows part of America.

Portuguese navigators began trying to reach the Indies by sailing round Africa in the 1400s.

The first expedition to use this route to the east successfully was commanded by Vasco da Gama. In 1497, with three ships guided by a brilliant Indian pilot he had found at Malindi on the coast of East Africa, he sailed into the port of Calicut.

The harbour was full of Arab and Indian dhows, and Southeast Asian sailing ships called *junks*.

The Portuguese made maps, or collected them from the mariners of the Indies. By the 1540s they had reliable charts showing the coasts from Portugal to Japan.

The Importance of Maps

The explorers **and** merchants of Spain and Portugal tried **hard** to keep their charts secret. But rival mer**chants** from Italy, England, France and Holland sent spies, who found the quayside inns **where** mariners gathered. They listened carefully to the mariners' tales, and bribed chartmakers to draw copies of their masters' secret maps.

The merchants of other European countries were also organising expeditions of their own.

One of the first was an English expedition, led by the Italian navigator John Cabot. In 1497 he sailed **across** the Atlantic, where he explored what is now the coast of Canada from Nova Scotia to Newfoundland and its rich fishing grounds.

In 1523 another Italian mariner, Giovanni da Verrazano, led a French expedition to North America. He carefully charted the Atlantic coast of what is now the United States, from North Carolina northward to Maine.

At one point along the coast, Verrazano rowed a small boat into a natural harbour, 'a very pleasant spot situated between two hills where a very large river flows into the sea.' Today the harbour is called New York.

FACT BOX

In 1497, the Portuguese navigator Vasco da Gama became the first European to reach India by sailing round Africa. For him and his sailors, it was their first sight of *junks*, which had been bringing spices, gems and silk to Indian ports from Southeast Asia for fifteen or more centuries.

The Unknown Southern Land

A map of the world, published in Holland in the late 1500s. The green-coloured continent in its southern half is labelled in the Latin language. TERRA AUSTRALIS NONDUM COGNITA *means 'not yet known southern land'. This 'not yet known land' turned out to be several separate lands, including Australia, New Zealand, and Antarctica, as shown in the sketch map on the opposite page.*

If you had been at school in Holland in 1570, your teacher might have shown you a map of the world, printed in a new Dutch atlas.

Turning the pages, you would have seen the outlines of five of the Earth's continents – Europe, Asia, Africa, North and South America – looking very much as they do in today's atlases. You would also have seen the outline of a huge sixth continent in the south Pacific, with a Latin name – *Terra Australis Nondum Cognita* – which means 'not yet known southern land'.

The Dutch geographers had put it in their atlas because it was thought that there must be equal amounts of land north and south of the equator. No European had ever seen this unknown southern land. But the huge sixth continent must be there, waiting to be found. When it was, there might be a great wealth of

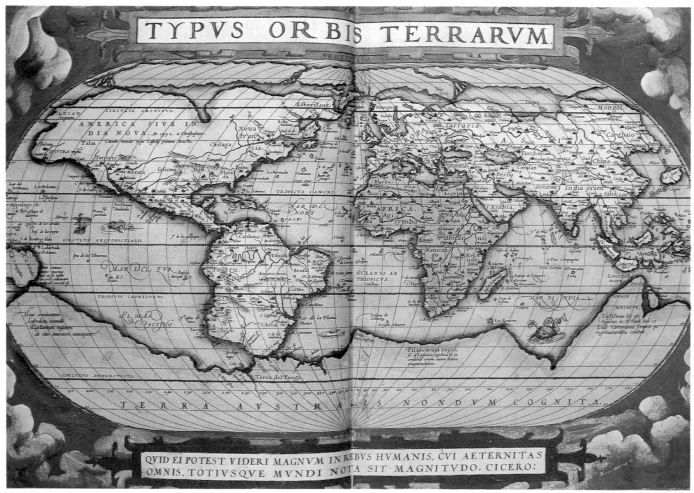

raw materials, and political power for the country that could dominate the land and the trade.

When, in 1606, the Dutch explorer Willem Janszoon found Australia, the geographers thought it was a northern tip of the missing continent. They believed New Zealand, reached in 1642 by the Dutch explorer Abel Tasman, was another part of it.

More than a hundred years later, the English navigator James Cook was sent to the Pacific to solve the mystery. Cook sailed round south Australia, charted the two large islands of New Zealand, and the icy fringes of uninhabited Antarctica.

Cook's expedition showed that south of the equator the earth is mostly sea. He sailed round the vast Pacific Ocean, reached many islands, and witnessed the skills of Polynesian mariners.

The huge sixth continent disappeared from the atlases. In its place, the mapmakers drew the first outlines of two smaller ones – Australia and Antarctica.

The English navigator James Cook.

Soldiers from all over the Roman Empire were posted to the wall.

About two hundred years before the ancient Greek geographer Ptolemy drew his world map, a Roman general called Agrippa made a map showing the Roman roads of Europe. His map is lost. But the well-designed roads are not, so Agrippa's road map – perhaps the first of Europe – can be reconstructed.

After the fifth century AD, the Roman Empire declined. When Rome itself was sacked by Germanic tribes in following centuries, the roads were used by missionaries and pilgrims, traders and other peoples who were migrating into Europe from Asia, as well as by armies bent on conquest.

FACT BOX

Using polished metal shields as mirrors to reflect sunlight, Roman soldiers could flash messages to each other over huge distances. It is said that on a clear day, signalling from hilltop to hilltop, they could send a message from Hadrian's Wall to Rome in a single day.

3 Into Asia: The Silk Road

A clay tablet map from Babylon. Drawn in the 7th or 6th century BC, it shows the world as a disc floating in the 'Bitter River', with eight outer regions inhabited by legendary beings.

FACT BOX

Led by Ghengis Khan, the Mongols from central Asia invaded China in 1215. His grandson, Kublai Khan, ruled a huge empire which stretched from China to Turkey.

Alexander the Great.

The oldest surviving maps in the world were drawn on clay tablets around 2000 BC, by the Babylonians, a people from western Asia. They were farmers and city builders who lived in the fertile valleys of the Tigris and Euphrates rivers in what is now Iraq.

East of the Babylonians, another farming and city-building people lived in the valley of the River Indus in what is now Pakistan and India.

Farther east, separated from the Indus valley by the highest mountains in the world – the Himalayas – was China. Here the ancestors of the builders of the Chinese Empire farmed the fertile plain between the Yangtze and Hwang Ho rivers. By about 2600 BC they had discovered how to use silk produced by silk worms.

North of China, in the vast spaces of central Asia lived a nomadic people called the Mongols. They were skilled horsemen, and lived in tents, following their herds of cattle, camels and sheep from pasture to pasture.

About 1500 BC another nomadic people from central Asia, the Aryans, came south into Persia. Together with the peoples already settled there, they built the Persian Empire. Over the next thousand years the Persian Empire had spread east and west by conquest. It included the Indus valley and Babylon.

Like the Romans, the Persians built roads. Using relays of horses, imperial messengers could travel between Iran and Turkey in a week – more than ten times faster than a trade caravan.

In 334 BC a Greek army, led by Alexander the Great, invaded the Persian Empire, and by 327 BC had conquered the whole of it. Alexander took geographers with him. Counting the steps of the marching soldiers to measure distances, they mapped their way to India and back.

Long before Alexander reached India, far to the east the Chinese had built a great empire. In 138 BC a Chinese overland expedition led by Chang Ch'ien reached Afghanistan. During

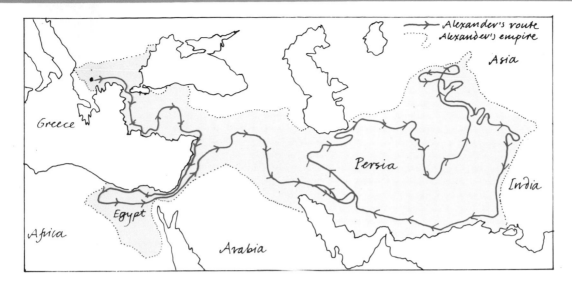

→ Alexander's route
..... Alexander's empire

Asia

Greece

Persia

India

Africa

Egypt

Arabia

their journey, the Chinese travellers saw fine horses, larger and stronger than those found at home. Paying in silk, the Chinese bought some of these horses, and took them back to their emperor, who was pleased. Thus a new overland trade route – the 9000-kilometre (5600-mile) long Silk Road – linking China and the ports of the eastern Mediterranean, was open.

Fourteen centuries later the Chinese Empire was ruled by the Mongols. And the Silk Road was one of its most important highways.

The Venetian explorer Marco Polo, the traveller with a notebook.

Along this road from Venice came a young Italian merchant, Marco Polo. He had left Venice in 1271, aged seventeen. He was twenty-one when he reached the court of the Chinese ruler, Kublai Khan.

Young Marco Polo impressed the Great Khan. He had learned languages, kept proper notes about his travels, and knew how to tell a good story. The Venetian worked for Kublai Khan for nearly twenty years. He was sent all over China, to the islands of Southeast Asia, and to Ceylon (now Sri Lanka) and back to buy the Khan the world's largest ruby.

Marco Polo wrote a book about his journeys, and the magnificent empire of Kublai Khan, where on New Year's Day, 'shall be offered by his subjects to the khan, more than 100,000 white horses'.

Many Venetians laughed at such stories. But Marco Polo's book would fill the heads of many

---

FACT BOX

The Chinese had large sea-going junks. Marco Polo made several voyages in them. They were used for trade with the sea ports of Asia, from Japan to Arabia, and with Zanzibar off the coast of Africa.

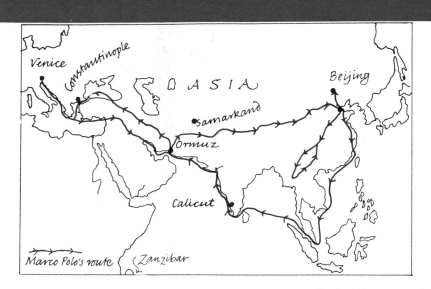

Marco Polo's route

Venice · Constantinople · ASIA · Beijing · Samarkand · Ormuz · Calicut · Zanzibar

young seafarers – notably one called Christopher Columbus – with thoughts of adventure.

In the 1500s Catholic missionaries, the Jesuits, began to follow explorers and traders along the newly discovered sea routes to the Indies. The Jesuits started to explore inland from the ports of India, China and Japan. They learned the languages of the rulers of the countries they visited.

Jesuits made the first accurate map of the whole of China. And on its western frontier, in 1689, they drew up a treaty between China and Russia. This followed the arrival in China of Russian explorers from Siberia.

Europeans were not always welcome. The Chinese emperors eventually tried to restrict and exclude them. In 1635 Japan was closed to foreigners. The ruler, the Shōgun Tokugawa, disliked the influence of the Jesuits and distrusted their missionary work. He wished Japan to retain its old ways and would only allow carefully controlled trade by the Dutch through the port of Nagasaki. Japan stayed shut for more than 200 years.

Tibet, ruled by monks, was also closed. But in the 1860s it was secretly mapped by Indian mapmakers. They entered Tibet disguised as pilgrims, counted their steps on prayer beads, and measured the heights of mountains with hidden instruments. The last large blank had been filled in on the map of Asia.

FACT BOX

Another visitor to China was the North African Moor Ibn Battutah, who set out from Tangiers in 1342. He also visited India. Like Marco Polo he wrote a book about his journeys.

4 Into Africa

In Africa there are footprints of a being that walked upright on two feet three and a half million years ago. They are the footprints of one of our ancestors. Some of the oldest human bones ever found come from the shores of Lake Rudolf in Kenya. This may be where the first humans evolved, from apelike creatures.

As their numbers grew, these people migrated over all of Africa. Some became nomadic farmers, wandering across the huge open spaces of central Africa. Others moved into the vast jungles of west Africa, or north into the mountains and forests of Ethiopia.

People also followed the River Nile, downstream into Egypt. And from Egypt, some of them moved into Asia and Europe.

In the fertile Nile delta about 5000 years ago, the people of Egypt made maps of their roads and the canals which brought water from the Nile to their fields. They traded with eastern Africa along the Nile and by sea.

Ptolemy's map shows part of Africa, with the River Nile in its proper place, but the positions of mountains and rivers in the middle of the Sahara on Ptolemy's map are wrong.

The Sahara became better known in the 600s, when Arab traders began to cross the desert from the east. They built settlements, like Timbuktu in Mali.

A thousand years later, Arab and African Muslim traders controlled the island of Zanzibar, off the east coast of Africa. European traders had settlements on Africa's west and southern coasts.

The traders came to Africa for gold, ivory, animal skins and slaves. They paid the African chiefs with whom they traded in guns, gunpowder and cloth.

The slave traders knew their way round Africa, but they had no reason to publish their secret routes. There were many blank spaces in the European maps of Africa, which posed a great challenge for explorers.

Long ago early peoples began to migrate from Africa to the other continents. Today nomads still travel across its great deserts, in search of pastures for their animals.

35

The Source of the Nile

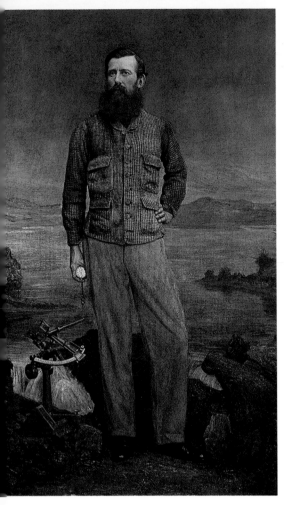

The English explorer John Speke.

The American explorer Henry Stanley finds the Scottish missionary David Livingstone.

One of the great mysteries of the geography of Africa was the source of the Nile. In 1770 the Scottish explorer James Bruce thought he had found it in Ethiopia, but what he had found was the source of the Blue Nile. The Blue Nile is the smaller of two rivers, which join to form the main River Nile in Sudan.

The source of the other river, the White Nile, was known to be much further south. German missionaries had seen snow on mountains in Kenya. Where did the water go when the snow melted? Arab traders spoke of a 'great inland sea'. Might this be the source of the White Nile? It could. In 1858 the English explorer John Speke was the first European to see it. The 'great inland sea' turned out to be a huge freshwater lake. Speke named it Lake Victoria. In 1862, Speke saw the Ripon Falls, the waterfall from which the White Nile is born.

Another famous explorer of the African interior was the Scottish missionary David Livingstone. He also wanted to stop the Arab trade in slaves and to open up trade routes favourable to Britain. In trying to do these things he found many lakes and rivers – including the River Zambezi and the Victoria Falls.

He was the first man to cross Africa from west to east. His efforts at mapping the interior were so successful that the Royal Geographical Society asked him to check Speke's discovery of the source of the White Nile. Livingstone set out in 1866. When he lost contact with the outside world, a Welsh-born American journalist and explorer, Henry Stanley, was sent to find him.

He did – in 1871 – and Stanley greeted Livingstone with the famous words, 'Dr. Livingstone, I presume?'

Livingstone's work inspired Stanley to continue it. Many others worked in Africa too, mapping the enormous continent. The last gaps were filled in the 1920s.

5 Into the Americas

When the first European seafarers crossed the Atlantic, and found America, they also found Americans – all the way from northern Canada to Tierra del Fuego, the southernmost island tip of South America.

Like all of us, these first Americans were descended from remote African ancestors. They had arrived via Asia. Thousands of years ago, hunters and gatherers, migrating slowly across Asia, reached the eastern end of Siberia.

Today the eastern end of Siberia is the western side of the Bering Straits, a sea channel which separates Siberia and Alaska, named after the Danish mariner Vitus Bering, who sailed through it in 1728. But about 12,000 years ago there was no sea channel. There was a land bridge connecting Asia with America.

By the time European explorers arrived across the Atlantic, the first Americans were farming and building cities. There were two empires – those of the Aztecs in Mexico and the Incas in Peru.

The Incas built a network of excellent mountain roads, linking their capital city Cuzco, three kilometres (nearly two miles) above sea level with the Pacific Ocean. It is said that relay runners could deliver fresh fish from the Pacific Ocean to the kitchens of Inca chiefs in Cuzco, many hundreds of kilometres inland.

Unfortunately for both of these empires, they were found by people who were more interested in gold than geography. Both the Aztecs and the Incas had plenty of gold. The people who discovered them had guns and gunpowder, which the Aztecs and Incas did not.

The Spanish conquerors, called *conquistadores*, destroyed the Aztec capital – the site of Mexico City – in 1521. They captured the Inca capital, Cuzco, in 1533. They shipped the Aztec and Inca gold back to Spain.

Lost and Found in America

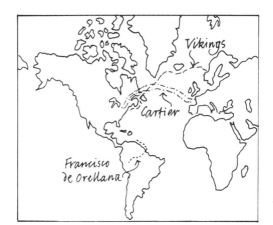

In Peru at about this time, was born the legend of '*El Dorado*', the golden one. At first, in the telling of the legend, El Dorado was a man – an Inca prince, perhaps – who was covered completely with gold dust and who had escaped the conquistadores. Later El Dorado became a fabulously rich city, lost somewhere in the jungles of South America.

The conquistadores' search for El Dorado had some surprising results.

In 1541, a one-eyed Spaniard, Francisco de Orellana, was looking for El Dorado. He was heading downstream in his boat on a small river on the eastern side of the Andes Mountains when he got carried away by the strong current.

He soon found himself on a huge river – the Amazon. Its banks were covered with jungle, from which people shot arrows at his boat. He survived and reached the Atlantic, to become – by accident – the first European to cross most of South America by river.

Far to the north, Jacques Cartier had explored the Canadian coast for France, looking for a way to the Pacific. In 1534 he entered the gulf of the St Lawrence River. The Labrador coast was so bleak he called it 'The Land God Gave to Cain'. Although Frenchmen who followed Cartier found no gold, they did find a source of enormous wealth – fur. French fur traders, with North American Indian guides and canoes, continued to explore Canada, where the Vikings once landed. The French also came south from the Great Lakes into Louisiana, and settled there.

The Vikings were the first Europeans to reach America. They are thought to have stayed at least one summer, somewhere on the east coast of what is now Canada.

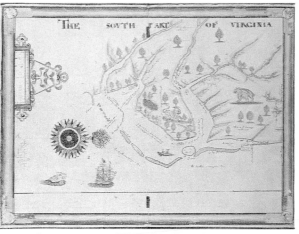

An early map of South Virginia.

In the 1600s English pioneers, in search of a new life, were building settlements on the east coast of what became, in 1776, the United States.

In the 1770s American settlements were becoming crowded. A million people had arrived from Europe by choice. And five and a half million people – victims of a cruel trade – had been brought from Africa in slave ships.

People began to migrate westwards, and in 1803 President Thomas Jefferson of the United States bought the Louisiana territory from the French Emperor Napoleon for 15 million dollars.

The President sent his secretary, Meriwether Lewis, and a geographer, William Clark, to explore Louisiana, and the mountains and plains that lay beyond.

FACT BOX

By canoe, horse and foot, it took the American explorers Meriwether Lewis and William Clark more than two years to cross the United States from east to west and back. They reached the Pacific Ocean in 1805.

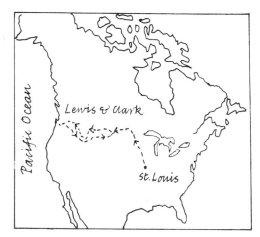

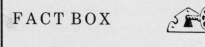

American President Jefferson sent Meriwether Lewis and William Clark across the United States.

6 Into Australia

Not far from Sydney in Australia, stone tools have been found. They were made by the first Australians more than 47,000 years ago.

These first Australians – ancestors of the Aborigines – arrived across a land bridge which joined Australia to New Guinea. Their ancestors came to New Guinea, by sea, from the islands of Southeast Asia.

In 1788 the ancestors of a new Australian people also arrived by sea. They came from England – more than 700 convicts, and about 300 seamen and soldiers to guard them. Few of the convicts were dangerous. They included seventy-year-old Elizabeth Beckford, who had stolen some cheese; thirteen-year-old Elizabeth Hayward, who stole seven shillings' worth (35 pence) of clothes, and eleven-year-old James Grace, who had taken some ribbons and a pair of silk stockings. In most cases these people had been starving and had stolen in order to eat.

These sufferers from harsh justice built homes in Sydney Cove, the first European settlement in Australia.

FACT BOX

A week's rations for female convicts on a ship carrying her from England to Sydney Cove:

Beef	28 ounces
Pork	14 ounces
Dried peas	1 pint
Oatmeal	1 pint
Hard biscuits	3 pounds
Cheese	5 ounces
Butter	3 ounces
Vinegar	¼ pint

Sailors were given twice these amounts. But these rations do not include fresh fruit and the disease scurvy was common.

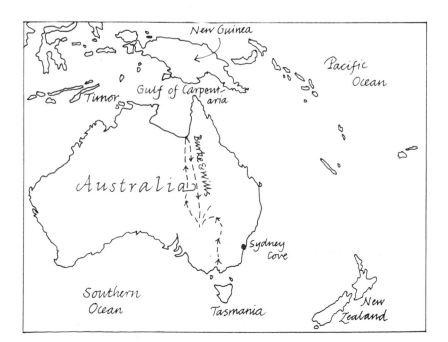

In 1861 Robert Burke and John Wills crossed Australia from south to north.

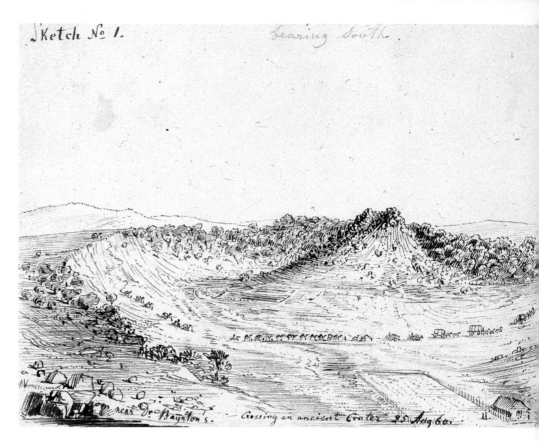

Sketch No. 1.   bearing South.

near Dr. Braynton's.   Crossing an ancient Crater 25 Aug 60.

The overland expedition of Burke and Wills crossing an ancient crater in August 1860.

During the early 1800s settlers came from Europe, by choice, to farm sheep, cattle and wheat. The discovery of gold, between 1851 and 1856, attracted many more people including American goldminers from across the Pacific.

Most of the settlements were on, or not very far from, the coast. Few European settlers had ventured deep into the interior, which Australians call the outback. They longed to know what lay there.

In 1860 Robert Burke and John Wills left Melbourne and headed north. They endured sweltering heat, lack of water and tropical storms, but were often helped on their way by friendly Aborigines.

The two men reached the Gulf of Carpentaria on the north coast in 1861. They were the first people to cross the continent. This triumph was lessened by the fact that both Burke and Wills died on their return journey.

7 Into Antarctica

James Cook had done some charting of Antarctica, without realising that it was a seventh continent. 'The risk one runs in exploring a coast in these unknown and Icy Seas, is so very great, that I can be bold to say, that no man will ever venture further than I have done.' Cook was wrong – but it was not until 1840 that an American expedition, led by Lieutenant Charles Wilkes, confirmed the existence of Antarctica.

In the first weeks of 1911, in the middle of the Antarctic summer, two expeditions landed separately on the edge of the Ross Ice Shelf, about 1450 kilometres (900 miles) from the South Pole.

The English explorer Robert Falcon Scott's ship, Terra Nova, *at the edge of the Ross Ice Shelf.*

The South Pole

A sketch by Edward Wilson who was on one of the first sledging expeditions, in 1901–3. The same sort of tent is still in use today.

FACT BOX

Early travellers never reached the Antarctic. It is still mostly unexplored.
Under the ice lies ten per cent of the earth's land surface.

One expedition was led by the Norwegian explorer Roald Amundsen, the other by the English explorer Robert Falcon Scott. As well as scientific and exploratory work, like others before them they both wanted to be first to reach the South Pole. Personal fame, and glory for their countries, were the goal. Both spent the following winter preparing their sledges and other equipment for the overland trek to the South Pole. At the beginning of the next Antarctic summer, both Amundsen and Scott set out southwards across the ice.

His sledges drawn by huskies, and using techniques learned from the Eskimos of Greenland, Amundsen and his companions became the first people to reach the South Pole on 14 December 1911.

Halfway to the South Pole, Scott sent his dogs back. He and his companions dragged their sledges themselves, believing that dogs were not reliable. They reached the South Pole a month after Amundsen. Weakened by hunger and cold, they died on their way back.

Yet again the exploration of an unknown part of the world had been successful, but at the price of lives. So what makes explorers explore?

One great explorer, the English climber George Mallory – who lost his life on Mount Everest – had an answer. When American journalists asked him why he wanted to climb the world's highest mountain, he answered simply, 'Because it is there.'

8 Into Space

Space exploration began when humans first gazed up at the night sky. Some of the oldest maps are of stars. For many centuries, travellers have used stars and planets to guide them.

Our world, planet Earth, is one of a family of nine planets. They are part of the solar system, which has a star we call the sun at its centre.

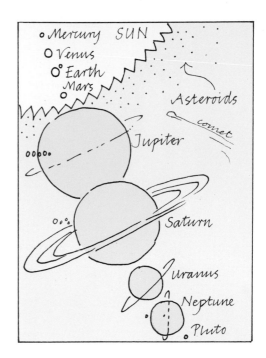

The solar system: a star we call the Sun, nine planets, many moons, and asteroids.

A family photograph of the giant planet Saturn and some of its many moons.

The space age began in 1957, when the Russians launched a spacecraft a little bigger than a football, *Sputnik*, into orbit around the earth.

In 1961 the Russian cosmonaut Yuri Gagarin flew one orbit round the earth. He was the first person to travel in space. And in 1969 an American astronaut, Neil Armstrong, became the first person to set foot on the moon.

The Russian Yuri Gagarin, who became the first spaceman

In 1977 the Americans sent two unmanned spacecraft, *Voyager 1* and *Voyager 2*, across the solar system towards the four giant planets Jupiter, Saturn, Uranus and Neptune.

The spacecraft carry television cameras. In the first twelve years of their journey, the Voyagers sent back hundreds of colour pictures of Jupiter, Saturn, Uranus, and their moons. The photographs are used to make maps of these planets and their moons.

Some of these places may be explored in the next century by people from planet Earth.

As you read these words, the Voyager spacecraft are leaving our solar system to wander among the nearby stars. Drawn on a little metal plate, attached to each spacecraft, a message shows where it comes from – our solar system – in case one distant day beings from another world are wandering too.

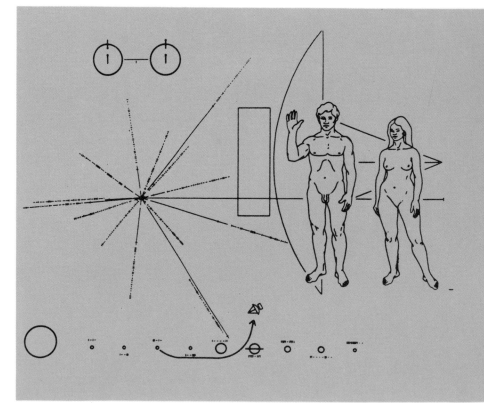

Above: Astronauts and spacecraft are launched into orbit around the earth by space shuttle. From orbit, spacecraft can be sent on journeys to other planets and beyond.
Right: Voyager spacecraft plaque—a message from planet Earth

Glossary

Aborigines The first inhabitants of Australia.

Amber Solid resin from extinct fir trees, found around the coast of the Baltic Sea. Used in jewellery.

Ancient Greeks The people who lived in Greece in the first few centuries BC and AD.

Archaeologist A person who studies early human history, often by finding and examining remains and ruins.

Aryans A people from central Asia.

Astrolabe An instrument used by navigators to work out where they are.

Astronaut A person who travels through space.

Aztecs A people who once ruled Mexico.

Babylonians A people who once lived between the Tigris and Euphrates rivers in what is now Iraq.

Cain In the Bible, the first son of Adam and Eve. He killed his brother Abel and was banished by God to a wilderness.

Celts In Roman times, a people of western and central Europe.

Compass A direction-finding instrument which shows where north is.

Conquistadores Soldiers and adventurers from Spain who conquered the Aztecs and Incas.

Cosmonaut Another word, of Russian origin, for an astronaut.

Curragh An Irish sea-going boat made of a wood frame covered with leather.

Dhow A wooden sea-going ship used by sailors from Arabia, the east coast of Africa, and India.

Ducat A gold coin used by Italian traders.

El Dorado A legendary lost city of South America.

Hourglass An instrument used to measure time. It is made of two glass chambers linked by a narrow channel, inside which sand takes exactly one hour to trickle from one chamber to the other.

Incas A people who once ruled Peru.

Indies The spice-growing countries of India and Southeast Asia.

Jesuits Christian missionaries.

Junk A wooden sea-going ship used by the sailors of Southeast Asia.

Landmark An easily recognised and well-known part of a landscape.

Mongols A nomadic people of central Asia.

Moors A Muslim people who lived in North Africa.

Muslim A follower of the Islamic religion.

Navigator A person who explores by ship.

Northeast Passage A sea route from Europe to the Pacific Ocean and the Indies, eastwards round the north coast of Russia.

Northwest Passage A sea route from Europe to the Pacific Ocean and the Indies, westwards round the north coast of Canada.

Outback Inland Australia.

Persia An old name for what is now Iran.

Phoenicians A seafaring people of the Mediterranean.

Pilot A person who guides a ship.

Polynesians The seafaring people of the Pacific Ocean.

Romans A people from Italy who once ruled much of Europe.

Shogun A Japanese military ruler.

Silk Road The overland trade route between China and eastern Europe.

Scurvy A disease caused by a lack of vitamin C.

Scythia In ancient times, part of where Europe and Asia meet, north of the Black Sea.

Sextant An instrument used by navigators to work out where they are.

Terra Australis Nondum Cognita (Latin) The 'not yet known Southern Land'.

Vikings A seafaring people from Norway.

Index